Anonymous

The successful business men of Newark, N.J

Anonymous

The successful business men of Newark, N.J

ISBN/EAN: 9783337713256

Printed in Europe, USA, Canada, Australia, Japan

Cover: Foto ©ninafisch / pixelio.de

More available books at **www.hansebooks.com**

INTRODUCTION.

 IN THE annals of history we have no record of a city which has taken the lead in the manufacture of every conceivable article as has the city of Newark. From the finest fabric of silk to the coarse iron casting; from the small pearl button to the immense steam engine— all of which conclusively proves Newark to be (as she is often called) the "Birmingham of America." Before proceeding to illustrate the "Successful Business Men" we would call the attention of the reader to a brief description of the city of Newark, which we have carefully compiled from reliable sources.

Newark was purchased from the Indians on the 11th of July, 1667, for an equivalent of $750.00. The area of the city is about 11,200 acres. The name was given by the Rev. Abraham Pierson, and was derived from Newark, Nottingham, England. The city is divided into 15 wards, and has 26 miles of sewers, 75 miles of water main, and 88 miles of gas main; a Board of Trade, consisting of 137 members; 15 Banks and 16 Insurance Companies; Real and Personal Estate assessed in 1871 at $85,986,241. In 1801 the aggregate product of the city was only $1,210,471; to day the manufacturing business of Newark is more than $90,000,000 a year.

The number of manufacturing establishments are 1,050, and the capital invested $34,407,670; the number of hands employed, 29,147; the amount of wages paid, $14,767,257, and the value of the products over $90,000,000, as above stated. This is by far a better showing in manufactures than New York City could make, and proves Newark's claim that she is not only the leading city in the State, but in the Union, to be a just one.

The leading articles of manufacture are: Boots and shoes, $3,000,000; beer, $4,000,000; enameled cloth, $1,500,000; clothing, $3,000,000; hats, $2,500,000; hardware. $2,000,000; iron, principally for domestic trade, $2,000,000; jewelry, a specialty of Newark, $5,000,000; leather, $5,000,000; refining and smelting, $2,500,000; saddlery and harness, $1,000,000; tobacco, $4,500,000; trunks and valises, $3,000,000, and varnish $1,500,000. Steam engines and machinery of all kinds are also extensively manufactured here, but like many other branches of manufacture we have no figures as to the amount, but the sum must be necessarily large.

The great secret of the growth and the prosperity of Newark is the low value of her building sites compared with those of New York, and her railroad communications with that city. There are five separate and distinct means of railroad communication between Newark and New York, and ninety-seven trains depart for and eighty-four arrive from New York City daily, exclusive of a large number of freight trains. The distance between these two great marts of the United States is only nine miles, occupying thirty minutes, and the fare only 15 cents. In addition Newark has the water facilities of the Passaic river and Morris canal, also that priceless boon, an honest city government and model fire and police departments; hence her taxes are consequently low. Her streets are the finest in the country, and Broad street the handsomest avenue in the world. The population of Newark is now about 130,000.

It is entirely unnecessary to add that the making of Newark what she is to day is due to its eminent business men, who by close application to and personal supervision of their own affairs, combined with integrity and honesty (not as a policy, but a principle), has been the basis upon which the firms here represented have built up their immense trade.

The world regards success as a test of merit. The lives of successful men are invested with all the interest of romance. The man whom the world trod upon yesterday, regardless of his merit, succeeds to-day, and to-morrow, in his turn, tramples on the world, which tamely submits to his imperious dictation. He is the same man still, only that he wears the jeweled crown and wields the potent sceptre of success.

How to win this regal coronet and sceptre is the great theme that engages all minds. The good strive for it that they may extend their influence in the cause of Truth and Morality; the bad, that they may revel in their own lusts. There exists no "Philosopher's Stone," but the secret is found in a careful study of the lives of our "SUCCESSFUL BUSINESS MEN," and nowhere better illustrated than among the eminently successful business houses of the beautiful city of Newark.

Every house we illustrate in this work will be readily recognized as the representative of its particular class, and many of them are wearing the crown and wielding the golden sceptre of success, with which their own efforts have invested them, with a commendable meekness, for the good of themselves, their fellows, and the great cause of human progress; and although some here represented have not yet grasped the golden sceptre, yet they are far up the rough and rugged road of fortune, where travelers are few.

T. C. V.

The Publishers hereby return their thanks to those gentlemen who have so kindly assisted them in the compilation of this work, and especially to Messrs. Hawkins & Dodge, machinery manufacturers, and to the editor of the *Newark Manufacturer*, for much valuable statistical matter which appears in the foregoing introduction. Also to Mr. Holbrook, of "HOLBROOK'S NEWARK CITY AND BUSINESS DIRECTORY," for the use of the fine engraving of Military Park, shown in this Work.

VAN ARSDALE & CO.

Respectfully
Seth Boyden

SKETCH OF SETH BOYDEN

THE subject of our illustration was an inventor of the highest order, and one of the great benefactors of our race, whose memory will ever be cherished by the American people. Born in Foxboro, Massachusetts, November 17, 1788, he removed to Newark in the year 1815. SETH BOYDEN's occupation in early life was a farmer, but, being of an inventive nature, he soon abandoned tilling the soil, and we next find him, at the age of 15, repairing watches. His first invention was a machine for making wrought nails, in 1810, at the age of 22. In 1813 he invented machines for cutting files, brads and machines for cutting and heading tacks. In 1818 a piece of patent leather —a military cap-front—of German manufacture, came into his possession, and he devoted himself to the production of a similar article, and in December of the same year produced the first side of patent leather ever made in this country. But, to give a list of the many branches of industry which Mr. Boyden brought to perfection, would occupy a larger space than can be afforded in this work. He was the pioneer in this country of brads for joiners, of patent leather, of malleable iron, of daguerreotypes, and of locomotives and steam machinery. He also greatly aided Prof. Morse in his perfection of the electric telegraph. His later years were devoted to horticulture. To his inventive genius belongs the credit of having aided Newark in reaching the enviable position she occupies to-day as a leading manufacturing city. Mr. Boyden died March 31, 1870, at the advanced age of 82, and his remains are deposited in Mount Pleasant Cemetery. He leaves a son and daughter, both of whom are residents of Newark.

Few men have lived lives of more unobtrusive usefulness, or been more regretfully remembered at death, than he. An elegant bronze statue is soon to be erected to his memory in one of Newark's beautiful parks.

RITCHIE & SON,

(Formerly Ritchie & Boyden,)
Late H. Ritchie & Co. & S. C. Thompson & Co.

MANUFACTURERS OF

Patent Padlocks,

FOR

Railroads,   **Stores,**

Safes,   **&c.,**

No. 15 Railroad Avenue,

NEWARK, N. J.

These Locks have been before the public for over twenty two years and have always given universal satisfaction in every particular. Most all the principal **railroads** in this country and Canada have adopted our Lock from the fact that they possess the essential characteristics of strength and durability. They are made of the best Composition for tough wearing strength, and contain no Iron, consequently they cannot rust; they are in every respect adapted to all out-door purposes where a serving and durable Lock is required.

A Sample Lock sent to R. R. Companies if requested.

Our Locks will be made to conform to any pattern of key on receipt of same by mail.

SUPERIOR

Wood Working Machinery,

MADE BY

M. B. TIDEY,

NEWARK, N. J.

MANUFACTURER OF

SPECIAL IMPROVED PATENT BOX & CABINET MAKERS' MACHINERY.

Established in 1844.

JOHN TOLER SONS & CO.,

MANUFACTURERS OF

Furniture Casters.

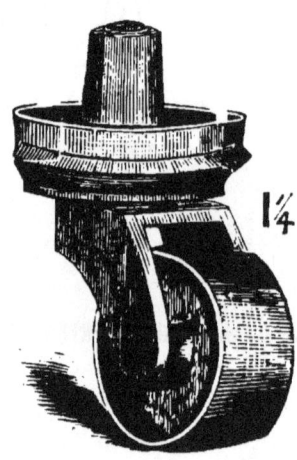

We make the greatest variety of any house in the States. We confine ourselves exclusively to their manufacture, and guarantee the quality. We solicit only the trade, to whom we are prepared to give the best prices.

NEWARK, N. J.

SOLE MANUFACTURERS OF

Wm. O. HEADLEY & SON,

MANUFACTURERS OF

Trunks & Bags.

No. 8 Warren Street,

Factory
Newark, N. J.

New York.

T. P. HOWELL & CO.,

MANUFACTURERS OF

PATENT AND ENAMELED

LEATHER,

*Bridle Leather, Sheepskin Skivers, Roans,
Harness Leather, Buck & Chamois,
Wax Calf, Oil Tanned Leather;*

ALSO

FANCY SHEEPSKIN MATS,

Cor. Wilsey & New Sts.,

NEWARK, N. J.

Salesroom, 77 Beekman Street, New York.

HEWES & PHILLIPS,

Engineers & Machinists,

MANUFACTURERS OF THE MOST IMPROVED

HIGH AND LOW PRESSURE STEAM ENGINES.
OF ALL SIZES

Steam Pumps; Sugar Mills & Sugar Estate Machinery; Lathes, Planing Machines; Hydraulic Lever, Screw and Drill Presses; Mill Rollers; Shafting. Blowers, Iron and Brass Steam and Water Valves; Steam Whistles of all sizes.

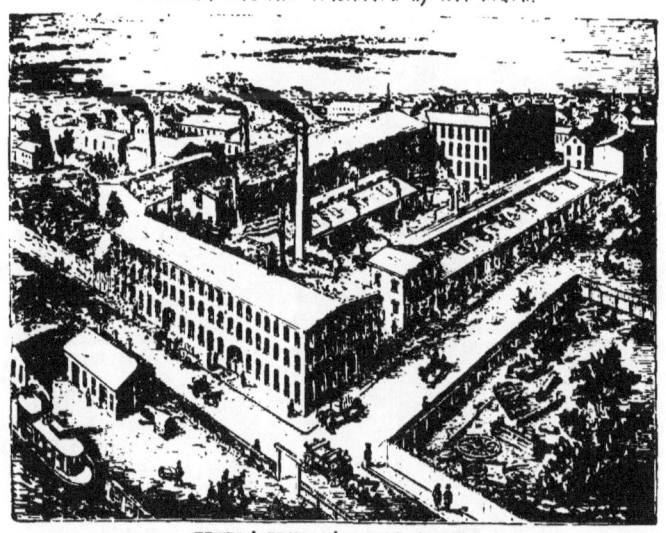

HEWES & PHILLIPS' MACHINE WORKS.

MACHINISTS' TOOLS,
IRON & BRASS CASTINGS OF EVERY DESCRIPTION.

STEAM BOILERS, OF ANY DESCRIPTION & DIMENSION PROVED BY HYDRAULIC PRESSURE.

Water Tanks, and all articles made of Plate or Sheet Iron. Also a complete assortment of Steam, Water and Gas Wrought Iron Piping and Fittings of all Sizes.

WORK AND MATERIALS WARRANTED.

Nos. 437 to 449 Ogden Street, Newark, N. J.

Orders and Repairing executed with dispatch.

J. L. HEWES, Passaic Ave., Kearney Township.   J. M. PHILLIPS, Woodside.

S. G. Sturges, Son & Co.

Saddlery Hardware,

84 & 86 MULBERRY STREET,

NEWARK, N. J.

Newark Steel Works,

Benjamin Atha & Co.,

Manufacturers of

Hammered and Rolled

CAST STEEL,

Newark, N. J.

R. J. GOULD,

STEAM FIRE ENGINES,

~ AND ALL ~

Fire Apparatus.

The third class Engine, with **IMPROVED VARIABLE PUMP,** *throws an 1 3-16 inch stream 265 feet.*

WORKS:

97 to 113 RAILROAD AVENUE,

NEWARK, N. J.

These Engines are used in New York, Brooklyn, New Orleans, Kansas City, Mo., Wilmington and Raleigh, N. C., Carlisle, Sharon, Wilmington, Del., Newark, Jersey City, Elizabeth, Orange, Camden, etc., etc.

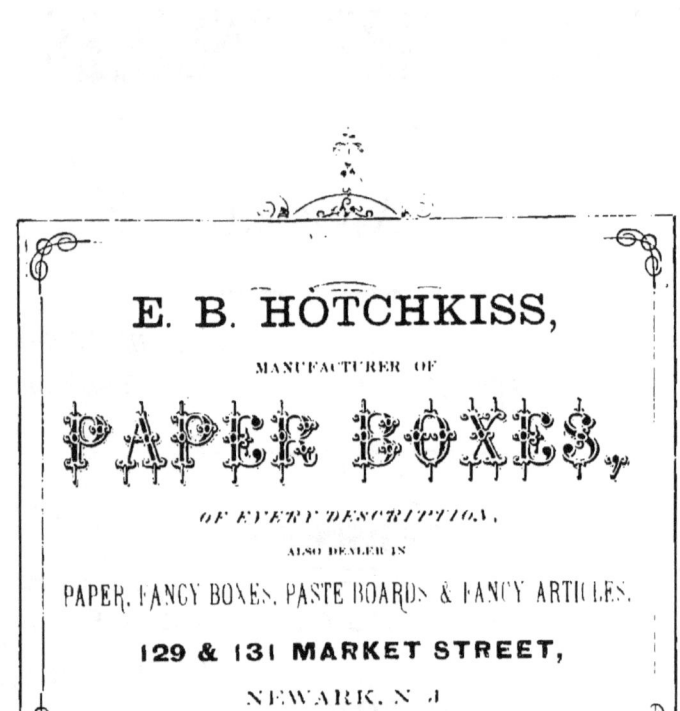

NEW JERSEY ZINC COMPANY

NEWARK, N. J.

AND

61 MAIDEN LANE, NEW YORK,

Manufacturers of

White Oxide of Zinc,

Zinc Paints. Spelter,

SPIEGELEISEN.

A. H. FARLIN, Treasurer.   *EDWARD BAKER,* President.

MILITARY PARK, NEWARK, N. J.

CANFIELD, JONES & CO.,

CELEBRATED

Boots & Shoes,

FOR GENTLEMEN'S WEAR.

MANUFACTURED FOR THE

EASTERN, WESTERN AND SOUTHERN MARKETS,

301 Market St.,

NEWARK, NEW JERSEY.

M. B. CANFIELD.
PHINEAS JONES,

IRA CANFIELD, JR.,
HENRY P. JONES.

WHEELER & ALLING,

Manufacturers of

FINE SHIRTS & COLLARS,

No. 209 MARKET STREET,
(Corner Beaver Street.)

NEWARK, N. J.

CHAS. W. WHEELER,
FRED. A. ALLING.

E. A. CROSSMAN, JR.,

Manufacturer of

FINE ROAD, COACH & TRACK

At Wholesale & Retail,

No. 25 Railroad Place,

(WHEATON BLOCK,)

Near Market St., N. J. R. R. Depot.   Newark, N. J.

L. LELONG & BROTHER,

GOLD & SILVER REFINERS,

Assayers & Sweep Smelters.

Corner CHURCH and MARSHALL STS.,

NEWARK, N. J.

LOUIS LELONG. ALEXANDER LELONG.

CROWELL & COE,

IRON · STEEL,

"BURDEN'S" HORSE SHOES,

CHAINS,

Axles, Whole Circle Fifth Wheels,

Rasps & Files, Malleable Castings,

ANVILS, VICES, BELLOWS,

Carriage Bolts, Carriage Hardware,

106 & 108 Mulberry St.,

Cor. Clinton Street,

Newark, N. J.

JOSEPH G. CROWELL.   JAMES A. COE.

Skinner, Leary & Lindsley,
Machinery in General,
23, 25 & 27 Lawrence St., Newark, N. J.

STATIONARY AND PORTABLE STEAM ENGINES,
Hoisting and Pile-Driving Engines, with Frictional Gearing,
Derricks and Contractors' Machinery,
Freight and Passenger Elevators, for Factories, Stores, &c.
Shafting, Hangers, Pullies, &c., constantly on hand or made to order.

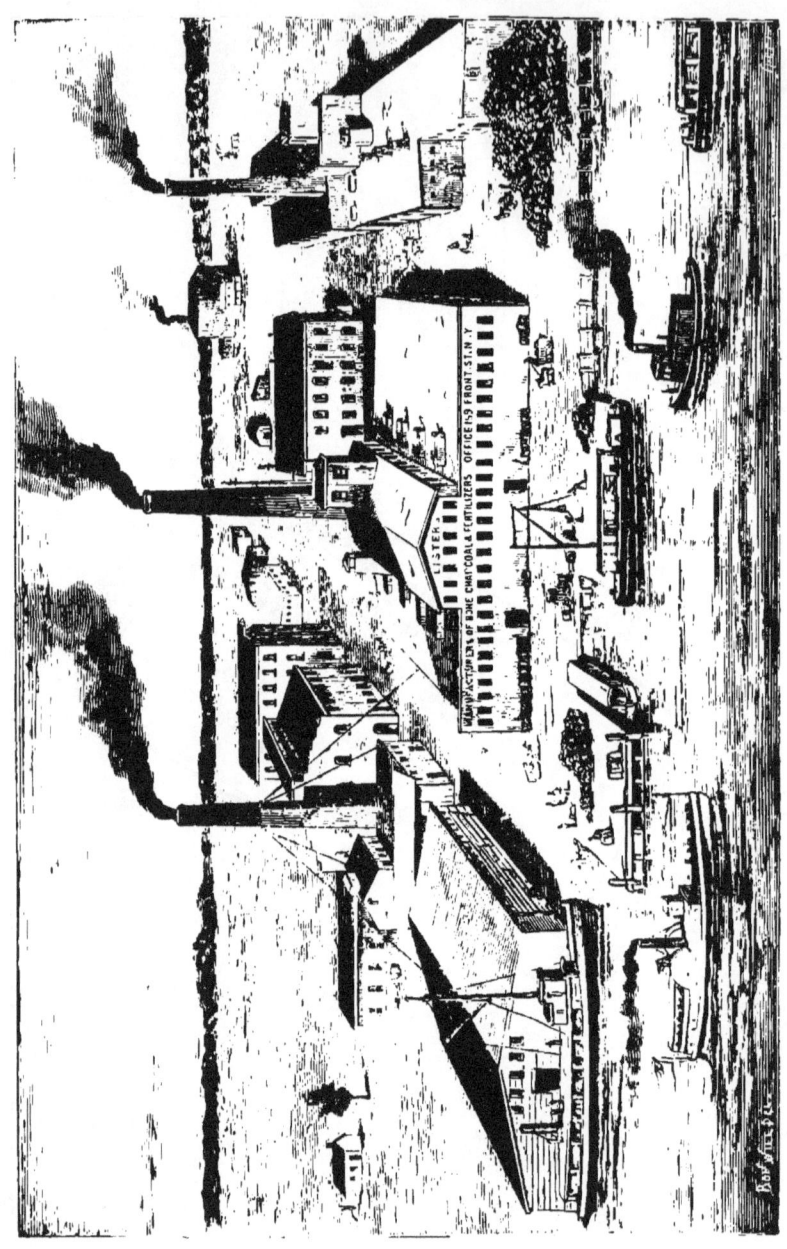

Passaic Carbon Works.

ESTABLISHED 1850.

LISTER BROTHERS,

MANUFACTURERS OF

IVORY BLACK,

Refiners' Animal Charcoal,

Pure Ground Bone,

BONE MEAL, BONE FLOUR,

AND

FRESH BONE SUPERPHOSPHATE OF LIME,

Bone Ash, Tallow, Glue, Glue Substitute, &c.

Principal Office and Factory,

Newark, N. J.

BRANCH OFFICE
159 FRONT STREET, N. Y.

THE illustration given on page thirty, of the Passaic Carbon Works, represents the largest and most extensive manufactory of the kind in the United States, and although the buildings already occupied cover a large area of ground, yet the Messrs. LISTER contemplate extensive additions the coming year to enable them to fill the constantly increasing demands for their manufactures. The products of this firm are Animal Charcoal, Ivory Black, Ground Bone, Super-Phosphate of Lime, Tallow, Glue, etc., and find a market for their sale in all parts of this country and Europe. The works are situated on the banks of the Passaic river, and have the facilities of the same for direct shipment by boat, in addition to which teams are constantly employed, and the many railroads to and from this city extensively patronized by large shipments to all parts of the country. Probably the sales of no branch of manufacture in the city of Newark are as extensive as those of the Passaic Carbon Works. The principal office of Lister Brothers is at the Factory in the city, but for the better accommodation of their foreign trade they have a branch office at No. 159 Front street, New York.

STAIR RODS,

Fine Silver and Gold Plated, Bronze, Nickel and Brass,

with PATENT adjustable Fastenings.

ORNAMENTED DOG COLLARS,

Patent Metalic Bridle Fronts,

The cheapest and most durable ever offered to the trade,

BRASS GOODS

Of any description made to order, or estimates furnished.

W. T. & J. MERSEREAU,

Salesroom, 62 Duane Street, N. Y.

Factory,
27 R. R. Avenue, Newark, N. J.

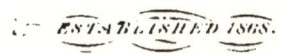

J. R. DENMAN,

BENT & BEVELED

Carriage Glass Works,

71, 73 & 75 BARBARA ST.,
NEWARK, N. J.

Clarence, Coupe & Hearse Glass,

AT SHORT NOTICE.

THE LARGEST CARRIAGE GLASS WORKS IN THE UNITED STATES.

ALSO MANUFACTURERS OF

Brilliant Cut and Ground Glass,

FOR DWELLINGS, &c.,

Money Openings, Shelves, For Banks, Rails,

And Desk Weights, Offices, &c.

SEND PHOTOGRAPHS & FOR CIRCULARS

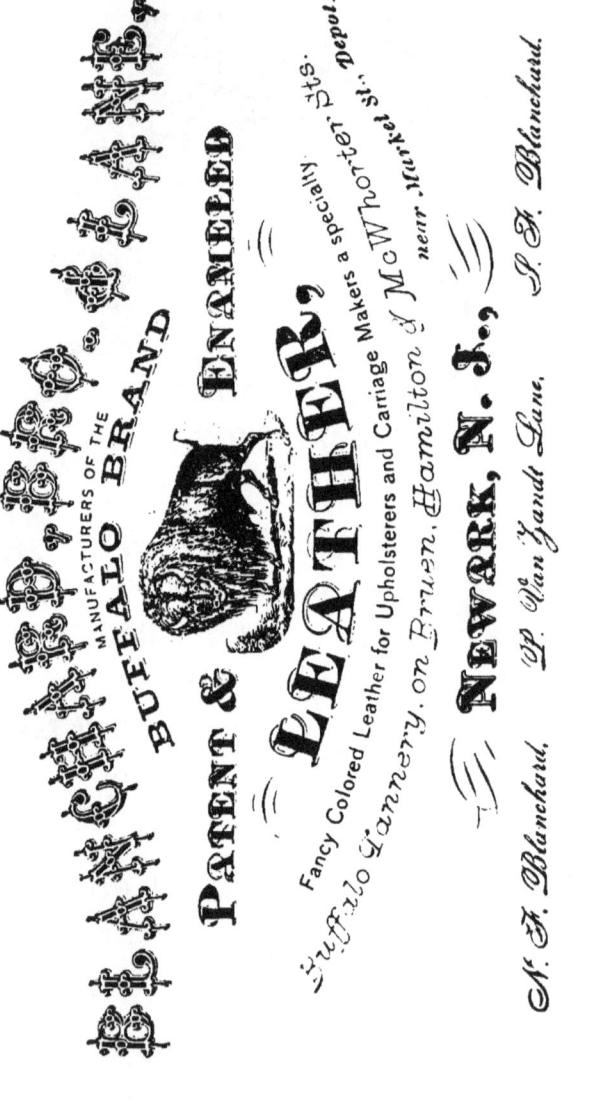

NEW JERSEY WIRE MILL.

HENRY ROBERTS.

MANUFACTURER OF

Steel and Iron Wire,

MARKET & STONE WIRE,

Bright and Annealed
Telegraph Wire,
Coppered Pail Bail,
Rivet, Screw, Buckle,
Spring, Umbrella, Bridge,
Fence, Broom, Brush,
and Tinners' Wire

WIRE STRAIGHTENED AND CUT TO ANY LENGTH REQUIRED.

Wire Mill, N. J. R. R. Ave.,
Opposite Chestnut St., Depot,

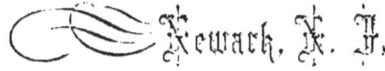
Newark, N. J.

Trains leave New York (Cortlandt Street Ferry) every hour for Newark.

Sargeant Manufacturing Co.,

← MANUFACTURERS OF →

Saddlery Hardware

Magruder's Pad Hooks, and Terrets, Gillett's Loop Pad Hooks.

Sargeant's Coach Pads, Gig Saddles, All Grades.

In Gold, Silver, Nickel, X. C. Japanned,
and Japanned and Lined,

Also Sole Manufacturers of

Sargeant's Novelty Gig Trees,

AND

Cole's Wedge-Tongue Trace Buckles,

75, 77 & 79 Summit Street,

Near New Street,

Newark, N. J.,

JOHN GEIGER,

MANUFACTURER OF

Files and Rasps,

Cor. Commerce St., and R. R. Place,

NEWARK, N. J.

Files and Rasps of all kinds Re-cut Warranted.

R. Heinisch's Sons,

MANUFACTURERS OF THEIR

CELEBRATED AMERICAN

SHEARS,

SCISSORS AND TRIMMERS.

Latest Patent Improved 1863.

WARRANTED THE BEST IN THE WORLD.

ALSO

THE CELEBRATED HEINISCH RAZORS,

Of every description.

Office and Salesroom,

No. 301 BROADWAY,

New York.

MANUFACTORY,
Cor. Bank, Silk & Henry Sts., Newark, N. J.

Newark Nickel Plating Works.

42 Mechanic Street,

NEWARK. N. J.

L. A. SMITH, Proprietor.

PROMPT ATTENTION GIVEN TO

Surgical Instruments,
STEAM FIRE ENGINES,
SADDLERY HARDWARE,
MILITARY MOUNTINGS,
RAIL ROAD CAR WORK, &c.,

Fire and Electro Silver Plater,

(MAKES A SPECIALTY OF)

PLUMBERS' MATERIAL, ALE PUMPS,
SODA FOUNTAINS, &c.

Licensed by the United Nickel Company of New York.

TOMPKINS & MANDEVILLE,

Wholesale Manufacturers of

COACH, CARRIAGE & BUGGY

HARNESS

Track Harness a Specialty,

323 MARKET ST.,

W. L. TOMPKINS,
D. V. MANDEVILLE,

Newark, N. J.

H. SAUERBIER & SONS,

MANUFACTURERS OF
SADDLERS', HARNESS, TRUNK, TRIMMERS, TANNERS, SHOE MAKERS' AND CURRIERS'

Machinery for Leather, &c.,

ALSO MANUFACTURERS OF
THE CELEBRATED

KNOX FLUTING MACHINES,

No. 0, 8 inch; No. 1, 6 inch; No. 2, 4 inch.

EXTRA ROLLERS FURNISHED TO EACH MACHINE.

Plain.   Nos. 10, 12, 15, 18, 21, 24, 27, 30, 35, 40.
Straight Diamond, " 10, 12, 15, 18, 21, 24, 27, 30, 35, 50

ALSO CONCAVE, DIAMOND OR TRIANGLE,

ALSO HAIR CRIMPERS.
34, 36 and 38 MECHANIC STREET,
NEWARK, N. J.

HENRY SAUERBIER,   HENRY SAUERBIER, JR.,   THEODORE SAUERBIER

LEATHER

FOR THE TRADE IN

Trunks,
Bags,
Satchels,
Carriage,
Harness,
Collars,
Book Binding,
Pocket Books,
Shawl straps,
Brushes,
Skates, &c., &c.

Manufactured by

Palmer & Smith,

No. 67 HAMILTON STREET,

TANNERS CURRIERS AND JAPANNERS.

EDWARD SIMON,
SAM. SIMON,

WM. SIMON.
M. SCHWERIN.

Edward Simon & Bros.
MANUFACTURERS OF

TRUNKS, BAGS & VALISES,

No. 64 Reade Street,

Factory, Newark, N. J.   **NEW YORK.**

The Messrs. SIMON have recently erected in this city, the elegant large four story Brick Factory, which we illustrate upon the opposite page. It is situated on Main street, near East Ferry Street Station, on the Newark and New York Rail Road. The building has a frontage of one hundred feet on both Main and St. Francis streets, with a depth of two hundred feet from street to street. It covers 12,800 feet of ground and contains 65,500 square feet of roofing, 460 openings, and will accomodate one thousand workmen. The walls contain eighty thousand brick. The building is heated with steam, and twelve thousand feet of coiled iron pipe is used for that purpose.

The brick Engine and Boiler House adjoining the Factory, is of the dimensions of 28x40 feet, and contains one of Watts, Campbell & Co's best fifty horse-power engines. The Mill Building is contructed of wood, three stores high, 36x100 feet.

C. H. & J. D. HARRISON,

MANUFACTURERS OF

Patent Enameled Leather,

ALSO A FULL ASSORTMENT OF TRUNK STOCK,

NEW YORK AVE., NEAR RAIL ROAD AVE.

NEWARK, N. J.

JOSEPH J. SPURR,

STEAM,

Marble and Brown Stone Works.

253, 255, 257 and 259 MARKET STREET,

NEWARK, N. J.

Marble Mantels. Monuments. Tombs. Grave Stones. &c., &c.

Also, Granite Monuments. Cemetery Posts. &c.

Newark Rubber Clothing Works.

L. JOY & CO.,

MANUFACTURERS OF

Rubber Clothing

OF ALL KINDS,

Piano Covers, Horse Covers, Embossed Rubber,
Carriage Drills, Wagon Aprons, etc.,

Nos. 56 to 66 Searing Street,

(REAR 184 WARREN-ST.,)

NEWARK, N. J.

NEWARK PAINT WORKS.

—

ISRAEL BALDWIN,

MANUFACTURER OF AND WHOLESALE DEALER IN

PAINTS, COLORS,

VARNISHES,

STAG'S HEAD WHITE LEAD AND ZINC PAINTS.

No. 362 PLANE STREET,

NEWARK, N. J.

HAWKINS & DODGE,
General Machinists & Engineers,
52, 54, 56 Morris & Essex Railroad Avenue,

make to order Machinery of all kinds, Patterns and Models, at reasonable prices and with dispatch.

HORIZONTAL, STATIONARY STEAM ENGINES,
(WITH OR WITHOUT VARIABLE CUT-OFF,)

from ten to one hundred horse-power, combining all the valuable and most approved features, viz: strength, durability, economy of steam, ease of access, steadiness of motion, simplicity, and symmetry of design.

Compact Vertical Engines,
from two to twenty horse-power.

PORTABLE AND HOISTING ENGINES.

STEAM AND HAND PUMPS,
simple in construction, thoroughly and carefully made, constantly on hand.

Shafting, Pulleys and Hangers,
with patent sleeve couplings, and adjustable self-oiling Boxes; also, an assortment of counter-shaft hangers.

POWER, SCREW AND LEVER PRESSES
of various sizes and designs.

MILLING AND DRILLING MACHINES, HAND LATHES, &C.

HALL'S MITER CUTTER,
for Pictures Frames and Door Mouldings.

CROSBY'S BLIND-WIRING MACHINES,
and other Wood-Working Machinery.

KIMBALL'S LOW-WATER INDICATOR,
for Steam Boilers, as certain in its action as the laws of gravitation.

ALSO, AGENTS FOR THE CELEBRATED

Tanite Emery Wheel,

Jobbing of all kinds will be promptly attended to at fair prices, and special attention given to the perfecting and building of

EXPERIMENTAL MACHINERY.

In the use of the best tools and facilities, employing the best skilled labor, and giving the work their own personal supervision, HAWKINS & DODGE are enabled to guaranty all machinery manufactured by them to be of the highest standard of workmanship, and at the very minimum of cost.

WM. HAWKINS.   WM. FOSTER DODGE.

CARTER, HOWKINS & DODD'S JEWELRY MANUFACTORY, NEWARK, N. J.

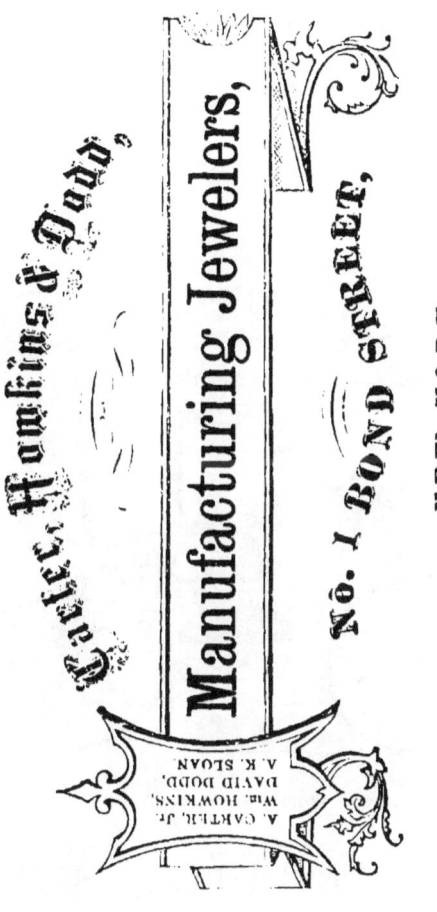

J. M. QUINBY & CO.,

No. 836 Broad Street,

Next Door to Newark & New York R. R. Depot.

HAVE IN STOCK AND BUILD TO ORDER

Hearses, Clarences, Coaches,

Light Road Wagons, &c.,

Warranted equal to the best New York make in style, material and workmanship.

MANUFACTURERS OF

Gentlemen's Fine Boots & Shoes,

206 & 208 MARKET STREET.

Newark, N. J.

ALL of our Goods are manufactured with especial reference to the Retail Trade. Our new and **IMPROVED LAST** *has met with universal favor and success, and is now pronounced by many prominent dealers to be the most perfect and easy fitting Last in use, and in order to overcome the trouble so long experienced in making to measure we furnish six different widths to each size, thereby enabling all who keep a full line of our goods to fit any ordinary foot.*

Always endeavoring to keep the style and quality of our goods equal to any in the market, we hope to be still favored with the liberal patronage of the trade.

NEWPORT COMBINATION TRUNK.

H. W. POINIER,

MANUFACTURER OF

LADIES' & GENTS'

TRAVELING BAGS,

SOLE-LEATHER AND WOOD

TRUNKS,

Shawl and Sling Straps in all Varieties,

Also Sole Proprietor & Manufacturer of the

NEWPORT COMBINATION TRUNK,

12 & 14 BEAVER ST.,

NEWARK, N. J.

PASSAIC SAW WORKS.

RICHARDSON BROTHERS,

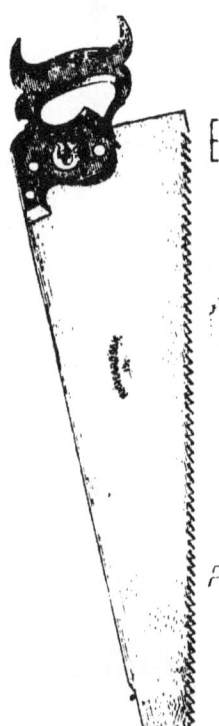
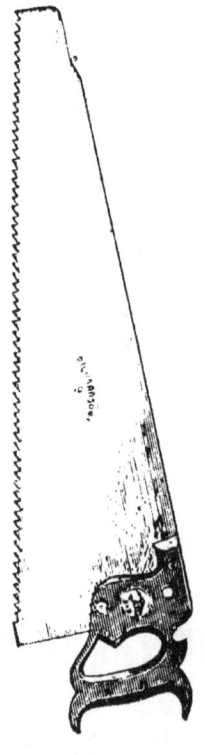

MANUFACTURERS OF

EXTRA CAST STEEL,

Circular, Mill,

Mulay, Cut,

Go. Back,

Bolting,

PRUNING, COMPASS

AND EVERY OTHER DE-
SCRIPTION OF

SAWS,

Cor. R. R. Place & Commercial-St.

[Established 1842]

Cyrus Currier's

MACHINE WORKS,

IRON AND BRASS FOUNDRY,

Newark, N. J.

Manufactures Steam Engines,

Fourdrinier & Cylinder  Paper Machines,

PAPER, FLOUR, AND SAW MILL MACHINERY,

OF ALL KINDS.

A large assortment of Mill Gearing, Pulley and other Patterns, (the accumulation of thirty years' business.)

SOLE MANUFACTURER OF

KINGSLAND'S PATENT BEATING ENGINES,

recommended after trial by most of the large manufacturers of paper as a decided improvement over the old method of beating pulp, doing better work with less attention and power.

ONE PATENT ENGINE

of thirty inches diameter is capable of doing as much work as four of the ordinary engines with Rolls 28 inches diameter and 30 inch face.

KEPT IN ORDER AT LESS EXPENSE,

and put in at less than one-half the cost of the ordinary engines necessary to do the same amount of work.

Have now upwards of ninety engines running on various qualities of paper, from wrapping to fine letter.

ALSO MANUFACTURER OF

BEACH'S PATENT BEATING ENGINE,

recommended to manufacturers of straw-board and straw wrapping paper; will reduce to half-stuff five hundred pounds per hour; requiring less than six horse power to do the work.

ATHA & HUGHES,

MANUFACTURERS OF

Enameled Carriage, Table & Stair

OIL CLOTHS,

IMITATION WOODS AND MARBLES, OILED SILK,

HATTERS' GLAZE, &c.

TRADE MARK
I. X. L.
AMERICAN ENAMELED
CLOTH.

WE present on the opposite page a view of the extensive factories, most of which are owned by ANDREW ATHA, and all of which are occupied by ATHA & HUGHES, for the manufactory of the line of goods specified in the above card.

This establishment is situated on Sussex Avenue, Newark, N. J., having a frontage of three hundred and twenty-five feet, and covering about three acres of ground.

There are fourteen buildings, two engines, five large boilers, five steam pumps, two enamelling, two calendering, and one sizing machine.

The founder of the house, ANDREW ATHA, commenced business on this spot in the year 1851 in a small way, but year by year enlargement has taken place until at the present time it is one of the largest of the kind in the world, giving constant employment to over one hundred hands, and preparing for the market daily about fifty thousand yards of finished goods.

The articles made at these works have achieved a world-wide reputation, and previous to our civil war were shipped to foreign ports. At the present time most of them are consumed in the United States and Canada. The present firm was formed in 1870. Their salesroom is at 56 Reade street, New York, where a general assortment can always be found, and orders for any amount promptly filled.

MANUFACTURERS OF CELEBRATED

American Horse Rasps and Files,

No. 73 New Jersey Rail Road Avenue.

DEPOTS:

ABRAHAM BUSSING,
   35 Chambers Street, New York.
S. O. LIVINGSTON,
   96 Reade Street, New York.
FULLER, DANA & FITZ,
   110 North Street, Boston,
JACOB UNDERHILL & CO.,
   118 & 120 Battery St., San Francisco.
HALL, KIMBARK & CO.,
   80, 82 & 84 Michigan Ave., Chicago.

JOHN B. KAAS & CO.,

Manufacturers of

COACH, CARRIAGE AND HARNESS

ORNAMENTS,

OF EVERY DESCRIPTION,

No. 250 Market Street,

JOHN B. KAAS,
ADAM KAAS.

NEWARK, N. J.

☞ CHASING, GILDING AND ELECTRO-PLATING.

ALL ORDERS PROMPTLY EXECUTED ON THE LOWEST TERMS.

ESTABLISHED 1850.

Newark Smelting & Refining Works.

Ed. Balbach & Son,

PROPRIETORS.

ALL CLASSES OF

Gold, Silver and Lead Ore Smelted,

LEAD BULLION AND CRUDE GOLD,

AND SILVER BULLION REFINED,

Office,

NO. 233 RIVER STREET.

Newark, N. J.

SEARFOSS'
Vertical Portable Grinding Mill.

For all kinds of Grain, Salts, Earths, &c. The Grinding surfaces are Burr Stone : the other parts are of Iron, simple in construction, strong and

FREE FROM ALL LIABILITY TO DERANGEMENT.

It is well worthy the attention of every person who uses such Mills.

THE FOLLOWING ARE SOME OF THE ADVANTAGES THIS MILL HAS OVER ANY OTHERS IN USE.

1st. Giving the greatest amount of product for the power used.
2d. Grinding the finest quality of meal, with the smallest surface of Stones passing.
3d. Less surface of Stones passing each other ; necessarily less speed required.
4th. Less speed required; necessarily less power need. The Bed Stone is rigidly secured in its place.
5th. The Spindle or Shaft of Running Stone rests on bearings, therefore the Stones can never get out of face with each other.
6th. Most simple in construction; therefore less liable to get out of order.
7th. The Stones can be re-set when worn up to casing; therefore more durable.
8th. The Stones can be dressed and the Mill set running by any one.
9th. It is the steadiest running, and the easiest regulated Mill in use.
10th. The Mill is made entirely of iron, except the grinding medium ; that is solid French Burr, or other stones as wanted.

An extract taken from the Record of the Eleventh Annual Exhibition of the New Jersey State Agricultural Society held in September, 1869, at Waverly: "To A. H. Searfoss, of Newark— The Committee speak most highly of a Portable Mill, for which they recommend a First Premium and Diploma."

At the Annual Exhibition of the New Jersey State Agricultural Association held in September, 1871, at Waverly, the committee highly recommended as combining all the advantages to be obtained in a Portable Grinding Mill, the "Searfoss Vertical Portable Grinding Mill"—the grinding surfaces of which are made of French Burr Stone, and dressed in the ordinary manner—and awarded to Mr. A. H. Searfoss a Silver Medal."— *Extract of Report of September, 1871.*

AMOS H. SEARFOSS,
MILLWRIGHT AND CONSULTING ENGINEER,

No. 362 Bank Street,   NEWARK, N. J.

Wiener & Co.,

Manufacturers of

All kinds of Leather-covered and Lined, Japanned and Lined, Silver-Plated, Electro Gold, Silver and Nickel Plated

Saddlery Hardware,

ALL KINDS OF

POLISHED AND PLATED WROUGHT STEEL BITS,

ALSO

Importers of English Saddlery Hardware,

N. B. Attention is called to our new and improved Leather-covered Harness Mountings, patented July 11, 1871, of which we are the patentees and sole manufacturers.

Illustrated Catalogues for 1873 furnished on application, to the trade only.

No. 87 Mechanic St.,

S. WIENER,
J. FEDER,
O. WIENER

NEWARK, N. J.

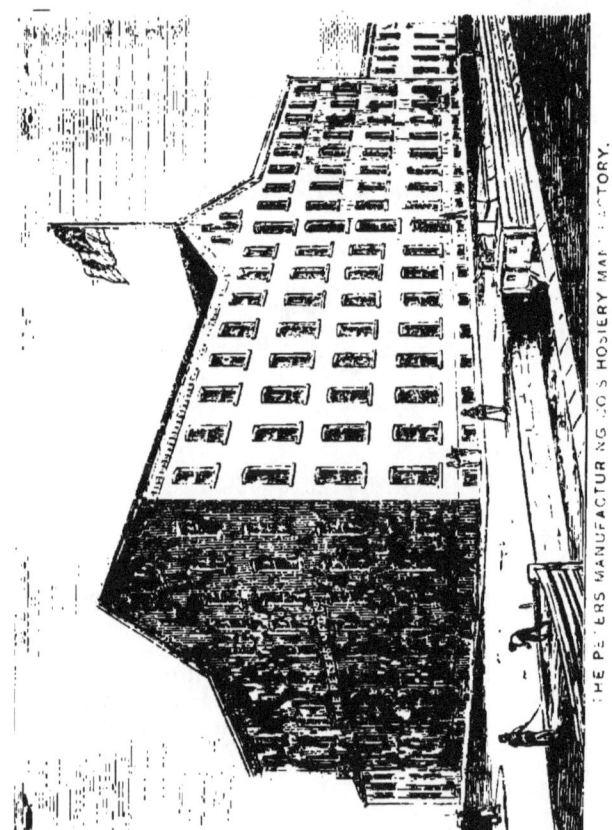
THE PETERS MANUFACTURING CO.'S HOSIERY MANUFACTORY.

THE PETERS MANUFACTURING COMPANY,

CORNER CHERRY AND CANAL STREETS,

Newark, N. J.

Manufacturers of

Under Garments,

FOR MEN, WOMEN AND CHILDREN,

IN ALL THE VARIOUS STYLES AND QUALITIES.

ALSO, 50 INCH AND 60 INCH HEAVY

SHEETINGS AND DRILLS

FOR OIL CLOTH MANUFACTURERS.

H. N. PETERS, Treasurer.

THE PETERS MANUFACTURING CO'S ENAMELED CLOTH MANUFACTORY.

THE PETERS M'F'G CO.,

Factory: Nos 579, 581, 583. 585 & 587 Market St.

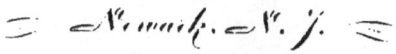
Newark, N. J.

OFFICE & WAREHOUSE: 124 & 126 CHURCH ST.,

New York.

Enameled Muslins, Drills and Ducks,

In all the various Colors and Widths.

Table Covers and Prints,

    Imitation Woods,

        Imitation Marbles,

            Stair Oil Cloths, &c., &c.

S. E. TOMPKINS. P. HAYDEN,

SAM'L E. TOMPKINS & CO.,

268 & 270 Market Street,

NEWARK, N. J.

UNIVERSAL TREE, No. 1.

NEW YORK TREE, No. —

HAYDEN & TOMPKINS,

79 BEEKMAN STREET. NEW YORK.

S. E. TOMPKINS, P. HAYDEN.

SAM'L E. TOMPKINS & CO.,
268 & 270 Market Street,
NEWARK, N. J.

ENGLISH EXPRESS TREE, No. —

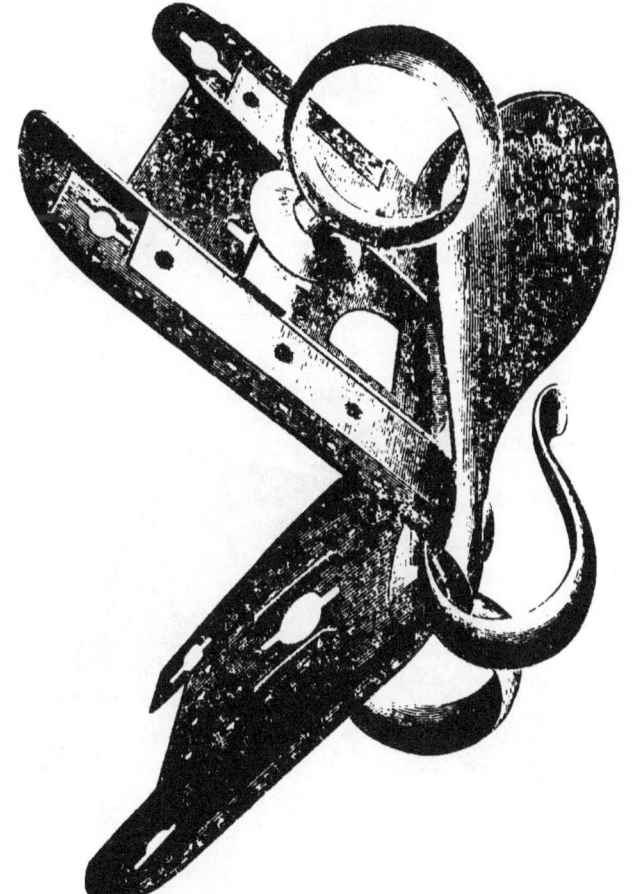

HAYDEN & TOMPKINS,

79 BEEKMAN STREET, NEW YORK

S. E. TOMPKINS.   P. HAYDEN.

SAM'L E. TOMPKINS & CO.,

268 & 270 MARKET STREET,

Newark, N. J.

UNIVERSAL EXPRESS TREE, No 4.

JAPANNED IRON JOCKEY TREE, No. 5.

HAYDEN & TOMPKINS,
79 BEEKMAN STREET.   NEW YORK.

S. E. TOMPKINS.   P. HAYDEN.

SAM'L E. TOMPKINS & CO.,

268 & 270 MARKET STREET,

NEWARK, N J.

JAPANNED GREAT WESTERN TREE, No. 11.

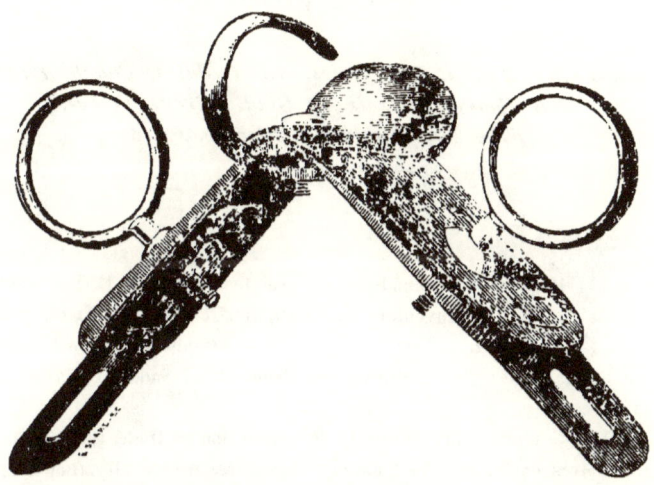

BOSTON PATTERN TERRET, No. 333.

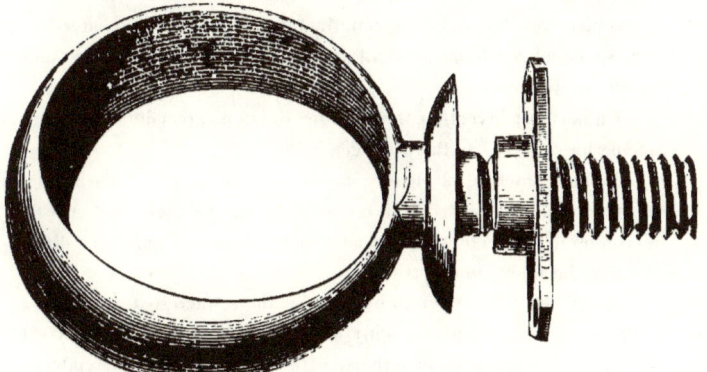

HAYDEN & TOMPKINS,

79 BEEKMAN STREET.   NEW YORK.

S. E. TOMPKINS P. HAYDEN.

SAM'L E. TOMPKINS & CO.,

Nos. 268 & 270 Market Street, Newark, N. J.

Manufacturers of and Dealers in

Saddlery Hardware.

*Tompkins' Patent Gig Trees, Gig Saddles, Coach Pads.
Bolt Hooks, Terrets, in Gold, Silver, Nickel,
Fine Tin, Japanned, Electro, &c., &c.*

THIS firm was founded in the year 1855, by SAM'L E. TOMPKINS, Esq., the inventor of "Tompkins' Patent Gig Trees," and although at first the beginning was small, it has now become one of the largest manufacturing establishments of Saddlery Hardware in the country.

Unlike many other houses in the same line of trade, they confine themselves exclusively to Saddlery Hardware, nearly all other large manufacturers and dealers combining Coach with Saddlery goods.

The introduction of "Tompkins' Patent Gig Trees" has wrought a complete revolution in the manufacture of Gig Saddles, and led to a corresponding development in all kinds of Trimmings used in the manufacture of Harness.

Unlike most Inventors, the Patentee found no great difficulty in introducing his "Trees" to the trade generally.

Being a practical mechanic; confident in the merits of the article he has produced; and gifted with no ordinary perseverance, he at once took a position in the trade which no adverse criticisms, or unforseen difficulties have been able to overcome.

Every obstacle thrown in his way by those interested in keeping his "Trees" out of the market, only seemed to develop and intensify his ability to meet and overcome them. His energy and power of endurance seemed to be almost unlimited, and no effort looked too great for him to make in his attention to demonstrate the practibility of his invention.

Such a man, moved by a true purpose, and accompanied with such energy was bound to succeed, and it was but a short time before the trade generally admitting the merits of his "Trees" commenced to adapt his improvement; and to-day, from small beginnings, we now see a business, of very large proportion, and there is scarcely a community, either in the States or the Canadas, in which the name of "Tompkins," is not as a "household word" in the Saddlery Hardware trade; and wherever known it is acknowledged that in all that pertains to his especial branch of business, he is the recognized leader. His fertile brain is constantly producing new ideas, and so maintaining the lead which he has obtained. Several imitations of his "Trees," have been presented to the trade, but *invariably* they have been based upon the peculiarities of his invention, and up to the present time the MERITS of his "Tree," have enabled him to distance all competition : and by this means endeavoring to avoid all suits at law, he has kept beyond all efforts at successful rivalry. In the Spring of 1864, PETER HAYDEN, Esq., of New York, (a name universally known and respected in the Saddlery Hardware Trade,) become interested with Mr. TOMPKINS, and since that time the firm has been recognized as one of the chain of "HAYDEN" houses, which are to be found in nearly all the large cities of the Union. The capital and influence thus added to the genius and energy of the inventor, gave a new impetus to the business, and from that time its growth has been of a very rapid character.

At the present time it is divided into three branches and conducted at three different places; at the same time, each branch is under the supervision and control of the active partner of the house. Mr. TOMPKINS, and all have sprung from the original firm as first established in this city.

Its principal manufacturing branch has been located at Ossining, N. Y., on the Hudson river, where it has all the advantages of river and railway communication. Mr. TOMPKINS gives to this department his immediate and special attention, and it is at that place that the large proportion of their manufactured goods are made. They employ some two hundred persons, and make all their goods from the foundation, having a malleable Iron Foundry, Machine Shop, and all the appointments of a complete manufactory. Their power being furnished by a fifty-horse steam engine. All the goods manufactured at that place are consigned to the salesroom in New York, and in this city, none being sold direct from the factory.

In this city they occupy the greater part of the large four story and basement, building located on the corner of Market and Lawrence streets.

The entire of No 268 and all of 270 Market street, except the store, being occupied by them. In this place they employ some sixty persons. This firm is noted for one peculiarity: that while many others discharge more or less of their employees during the dull seasons, this establishment but very rarely adopt that course, preferring to accumulate stock to discharging good workmen. This fact is so well known among mechanics generally, that it is considered as equivalent to securing constant work the year round to be employed by this firm. At this place the finer grades of their goods are manufactured: such as very fine Gig Saddles, Tompkins' Covered Trees, Jap. Seat, with Leather Jockeys, &c.

They also make a specialty of Fine Harness Mountings: such as Silver Plated, Gilt, Nickel, Covered, &c., &c.

The third and fourth stories of the buildings occupied by them are used for manufacturing purposes. The first and second stories with basement being devoted to show room purposes, and the general business of Saddlery Hardware, of which they always keep a large and well assorted stock on hand, both of domestic and foreign manufacture.

The immediate supervision of the store and factory in this city, as also their store in New York, is under the direction of Mr. JOHN M. GWINNELL, who has been in their employ for the last twelve years, and by his industry and attention to the interests of his employers, has risen from the workbench to his present responsible position, in which he has the full confidence and esteem of the firm.

Their principal warehouse is located at 79 Beekman street, New York City, under the name of HAYDEN & TOMPKINS. At that place they occupy the entire building, consisting of five stories and basement.

Here the purchaser can always find on hand ready for sale a large and well assorted stock of all their own manufacture, as well as a large and varied assortment of American and English Hardware, in which they do a large and increasing business, and although it is only three years since they opened this house, it has already established for itself a character second to none in the trade. The entire business of the firm is based upon the one-price system; fair dealing to all is a characteristic which they may well be proud of.

Intemperance in any of their employees is frowned upon, and every effort is made to have justice done to every one. That this is appreciated by their employees is evident from the fact, that there are but few changes ever taking place in their working force.

They were among the first to issue an illustrated Price-List, showing the character of their goods, with full description and prices.

Their Catalogue for 1872, was acknowledged to be the most complete ever issued, and received complimentary notices from the Harness Makers' Journal and other papers. Their Illustrated Catalogue for 1873, is now being issued, and it is very far in advance of the previous year, and is by far the most complete list of Saddlery Hardware ever presented to the trade.

This is so greatly appreciated by the trade generally, that in more than one case the general details of the book have been copied by others, and in one instance at least nearly one-half of the illustrations in a price-list issued by one of their competitors have been copied direct from their book.

Some idea of the vast details of their business may be obtained by reference to their price-list. It is a book of over two hundred and fifty pages, neatly printed on tinted paper, in good clear type, purchased for their especial use, and owned by the firm. It contains over one hundred and forty distinct illustrations of their goods. It gives prices and description of over six hundred (600) different styles, sizes and qualities of Gig Trees. If a sample of each size and quality of various kinds of articles, illustrated, and for which prices are quoted in their book, were laid out for examination, it would take over one thousand different Gig Tree Bolt Hooks; thirteen hundred Terrets; two hundred Post Hooks; two hundred and fifty Pad Hooks; two hundred Fly Post Hooks; one hundred and fifty Fly Terrets; three hundred Trace Buckles; four hundred Gig Saddles; two hundred Coach Pads; one hundred Patent Leather Winkers; together with a very large assortment of Gig and Coach Harness; Harness Buckles; Pad Plates; Bits; Rings; Fronts, and all the details necessary to a complete Harness trade. The illustrations as given in accompanying pages are as taken from their Catalogue, and they will serve to illustrate the character of their goods, and at the same time show the attention bestowed upon their price-list.

This house in its history is but another instance of the rewards that persevering industry obtains. And it stands out in bold relief as an instance of success obtained, not by chicanery and fraud but by strict attention to business and the observance of those rules which alone can give true character.

Industry, Sobriety and Personal attention to their trade, have been the rules which have governed them in their business visitations, and as a consequence the rewards of success have been given to them.

DOUGLAS, SONS & CO., Manufacturers of Fine Furniture.—Warerooms, 797 Broad St.—Factory, rear 797 to 817 Broad St.

— ESTABLISHED 1842. —

DOUGLAS, SONS & Co.,

No. 797 BROAD STREET,

Manufacturers of

FINE CABINET FURNITURE,

— FOR THE —

Parlor, Library, Dining-Room, Chamber, Church, Bank, Lodge, and Office.

DEALERS IN

Carpets, Oil Cloths, Cornices, Shades, Lambrequins, Mirrors, Wall Papers, Decorations, &c., &c.

Sole Agents for the

"**Webber,**" **Bacon** & **Karr** and other

First-Class Pianos,

ALSO, THE MASON & HAMLIN ORGANS.

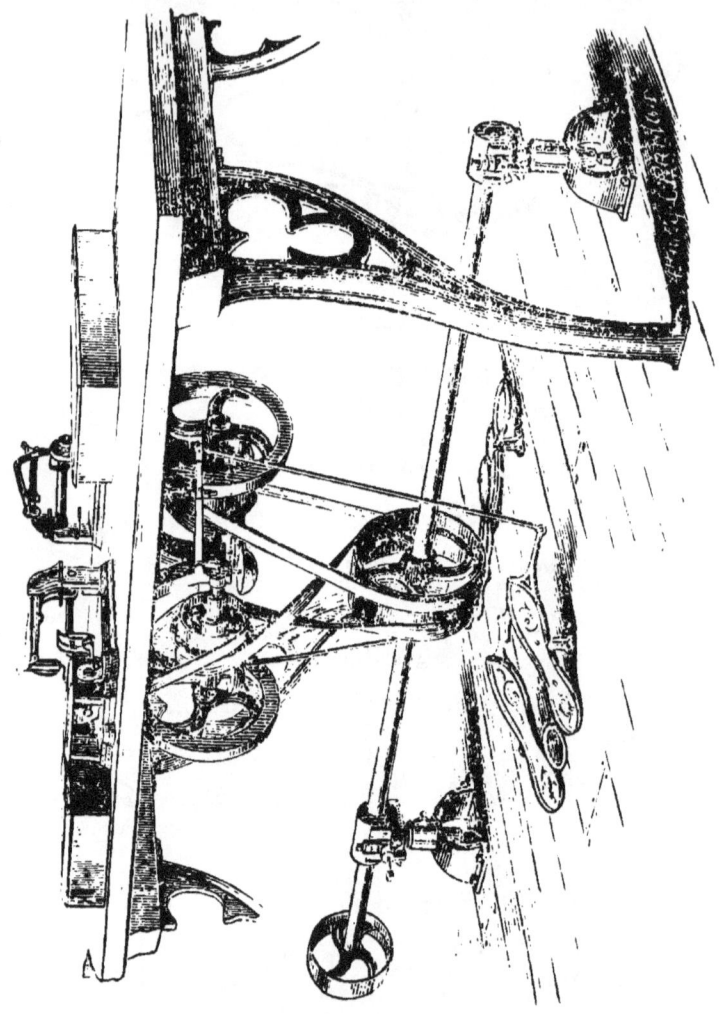

WHITLOCK'S
PATENT FRICTION MOTOR.

Set in Double Rows for running all the various Sewing Machines by Steam Power.

MANUFACTURED BY

Seymour T. Whitlock,

43 Lawrence Street.   NEWARK, N. J.

Sash Dove-Tailing Machine.

The accompanying Cut is a representation of a Machine long needed for the especial purpose of forming the Dovetail Joints universally used on the Stiles and Meeting Rails of Sashes. It combines all the elements of simplicity, occupies but little space and only requires the power of an ordinary saw. The Machine is so arranged that but a few minutes is required to adjust it, so as to cut with positive accuracy the various sizes and forms of Dovetails or straight Tenons ever used on Sashes and Blinds. After once adjusted to the desired form, the operation is so simple that the most inexperienced person can work it. All that is required, is to place the Stuff on the table, and then push it forward until it has passed the saws or cutters, and the work is done, making a more perfect joint (either coped or not as the case may require) than can be made by hand, with a saving of much time in the handling, as each joint (male and female) is produced at a single operation.

This machine is already extensively used, and has received the highest commendations. No shop (however small,) where power is used, can afford to be without it.

Seymour & Whitlock,

Engineers & Machinists,

Manufacturers of

Iron and Wood Working Machinery, Baxter's Portable Steam Engines, Shafting, Pullies, Self Oiling Hangers, &c.,

43 Lawrence Street,　　　　　　　　**NEWARK, N. J.**

S. H. PERRY, OX-BRAND

Manufacturer of the

Patent & Enameled Leather,

DULL & POLISHED GRAIN BAG LEATHER & SHOE SPLITS.

SOUTH ORANGE AVENUE, RICHMOND & NORFOLK STREETS,

NEWARK, N. J.

MILLER, McCULLOUGH & OBER,

Wholesale Manufacturers of

FIRST-CLASS

Men's Boots & Shoes,

No. 272 MARKET STREET,

Newark, N. J.

SHEPARD'S
Spring Bed Bottom.

Patented July 26th, 1870.

For EASE, COMFORT, SIMPLICITY and DURABILITY, we challenge comparison with any other Spring Bed that has yet been offered to the public for the same money. It forms a luxurious bed with but a single mattress.

IT IS PERFECTLY NOISELESS.

It is DURABLE. It is CLEANLY, giving no harbor for vermin. Can be put up or taken down by any one in a few minutes.

IT IS WONDERFULLY CHEAP, COMING WITHIN THE MEANS OF ALL.

Manufactured and Sold Wholesale and Retail by

MILLEN & JACOBUS,

30 WARD STREET,

Newark, N. J.

~{ Established 1835 }~

JOHN D. FITZ-GERALD,

Late D. PRICE & FITZ-GERALD.

MANUFACTURER OF

Fine Varnishes,

Japans, &c.

365 & 367 MULBERRY STREET,

NEWARK, N. J.

NEWARK POST OFFICE.

Mayhew, Leonard & Co.,

Manufacturers of

Fine Jewelry,

Rear 19 Green Street,

NEWARK, N. J.

HUNTINGTON MACHINE WORKS.—E. W. ROFF, Proprietor.

Huntington Machine Works

E. W. ROFF, Proprietor,

NEWARK, N. J.

MANUFACTURE

SHAFTING, PULLEYS,

—AND—

WOOD WORKING MACHINERY,

FOR CABINET AND BOX MAKERS.

SASH AND BLIND MACHINERY, MOULDING MACHINES, BAND AND SCROLL SAWS, CROSS CUT AND SWING SAWS, RIP OR SLITTING SAWS, PATENT VERTICLE RE-SAWS, CIRCULAR RE-SAWS from 24 to 66 inch, CLAP BOARD OR BEVEL SAWS, SPOKE AND WHEEL MACHINERY, IRON AND WOOD FRAME TENONING MACHINES, FLUTING MACHINES for Newels and Balusters, FOOT AND POWER MORTISING MACHINERY, &c.

135 & 137 Halsey Street.

Wholesale Manufacturers of

GENTLEMEN'S AND BOYS'

Fine Hand-Sewed

First Premiums.

CANFIELD, JONES & CO.

NEWARK, N.J.

Boots & Shoes,

No. 301 Market Street,

M. B. CANFIELD,
IRA CANFIELD, JR.

PHINEAS JONES,
H. P. JONES.

—— ESTABLISHED 1835. ——

Smith & Townley,

Late C. W. BADGER & CO.,

WHOLESALE DRUGGISTS,

AND DEALERS IN

CHEMICALS, DYE STUFFS,

PAINTS, OILS,

AND

MANUFACTURERS' SUPPLIES,

861 Broad Street,

(Opposite Fair Street.)

Charles B. Smith,
Wm. M. Townley,

NEWARK, N. J.

CHARTERED IN 1811.

NEWARK MUTUAL FIRE Insurance Company,

Office--741 & 743 Broad Street,

NEWARK, N. J.

ASSETS, - - - - - $500,000.00.

This Company being Purely Mutual, all the Profits belong to the Insured and Scrip Holders.

Policies issued for one, three or five years on either Mutual or Non-Participating Plan, at as Low Rates as will prove advantageous to the Insured and the Company.

LOSSES PAID PROMPTLY.

Your Insurance is Respectfully Solicited.

CEPHAS M. WOODRUFF, President.

JOHN J. HENRY, Secretary.

Amzi Pierson & Bro.,

FINE

Steam Printers,

Lithographers & Engravers,

STATIONERS & BLANK BOOK MANUFACTURERS,

No. 186 Market Street,

AMZI PIERSON,
CHAS. L. PIERSON.

NEWARK, N. J.

STYLE, DURABILITY AND ECONOMY.

OUR SILK HATS
... purposed to any in ... routine, and

Soft and Stiff Hat[s]
... timent embraces all ... standing new and novel designs.

... QUALITY AND PRICE
surpassing any other ... ishment in the Union. A full assortment of ... 'S & CHILDREN'S

HATS & CAPS.
... ticular attention given ... furnishing the little ones ... becoming Hat or Cap.

MILITARY PARK, NEWARK, N. J.

Ladies can always find a ... complete assort...

BONNETS
AND

ROUND HATS,
... trimmed and trimmed.

WITH

... BE ...

FURS AND STRAW GOODS,
IN THEIR SEASON.

Money refunded if Goods are not as represented.

COREY & STEWART,
711 & 713 BROAD STREET, NEWARK, N. J.

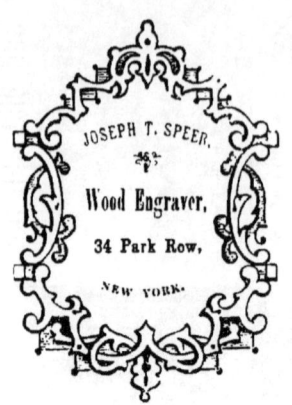